# CONSENT TO BURN

## WHO WILL YOU BURN FOR?

### AIDAN LAMBERT

# ENDORSEMENTS

It is a joy to write a few lines as an endorsement of Evangelist Aidan Lambert's latest book, "Consent to Burn." I have known and pastored Aidan all his life. Literally, I have been his Pastor from even before he was born. I have seen him in good times and bad, struggles and triumphs. However, I have also witnessed in Aidan an indescribable hunger for God and His Word, a compelling passion for the lost, and an unreserved surrender to God's plan for his life. His story is real, it is raw, but it is also life-giving. Allow the same God that has transformed Aidan's life to transform you.

Pastor Timothy Coats
*Lead Pastor, Family First Assembly*
Spring Hill, FL

# TABLE OF CONTENTS

# DEDICATION

To my beautiful wife, Faith Lambert.

You are the quiet strength behind every step I take, the steady presence beneath every word I write, the living reminder of God's goodness to me. I will never fully grasp the weight of your prayers, those whispered conversations with Heaven that lifted me in my lowest moments. I don't know how many tears you've cried when no one was watching, or how often you knelt before God with my name on your lips. But I know this: you prayed, and you believed. You challenge me to be more like Jesus, not by pressure, but by example. You pushed me to go deeper, to run harder, to chase not just the calling, but the One who called me. You are my miracle, my ministry partner, and the gift I will spend a lifetime unwrapping with gratitude. From today until the end of my days, I will love you, with every word, every breath, and every heartbeat.

# FOREWORD

I have had the great blessing of watching Aidan and Faith Lambert grow and develop as evangelists in the early days of their ministry. They have remained full of faith and fire! They have much to share in regard to abandoning all to follow the commands of the Lord and I believe this book will be a great blessing to you as you launch out into the deep to follow the same path boldly. This is not a cookie cutter, plastic, safe, church type of read. This is an authentic, raw, and transparent look into what it means to follow the voice of God.
Pick it up, and don't put it down!

Evangelist Levi Lutz
*Harvest Now Ministries*
*CfaN Bootcamp Director*
Orlando, FL

# CHAPTER I - THE ECHO OF EDEN

A vast, silent void stretched into eternity, an endless expanse untouched by time or form. Darkness reigned supreme, thick and infinite, yet it was not empty—for God presided over the silence with absolute, sovereign authority. He dwelt in unapproachable light, clothed in majesty and splendor, His presence filling the formless deep.

To His left stood the angels—radiant, awe-inspiring beings, each one a masterpiece of divine craftsmanship. Their wings shimmered like polished gold, their voices sang in endless symphony, lifting eternal praise to the One who formed them from glory. To His right stood His Son—Jesus Christ, co-eternal, co-glorious, the very Word through whom all things would be made. His eyes burned with love and power, and in Him the fullness of God was pleased to dwell.

God held all power, all dominion, and all majesty. He lacked nothing. No hunger stirred within Him. No loneliness gnawed at His heart. He was complete—perfect in being and beauty.

Yet even in the courts of heaven, amid the resounding praise and radiant worship, a shadow began to stir.

Among the hosts of angels, one shone brighter than the rest—a magnificent and exalted creature named Lucifer. He walked among the fiery stones; his garments gleamed with precious stones, and music flowed from his very being like a river of light. He was glorious, resplendent, anointed.

But the greater his splendor, the deeper his fall.

Pride crept like poison into Lucifer's heart. No longer satisfied to reflect God's glory, he longed to possess it. He gazed upon the throne and envisioned himself seated upon it. His voice, once raised in worship, began to whisper treason. In secret, he conceived rebellion—an uprising against the very One who had created him.

But nothing is hidden from the all-knowing God.

In a moment that shook the heavens, the truth was unveiled. The holy silence was shattered by judgment. With unmatched fury and unyielding righteousness, God rose from His throne, and with a word of command, He cast Lucifer down. Lightning split the heavens, and the morning star fell, hurled from glory like a dying flame. Alongside him fell a third of the angelic host—those who had dared to join in his rebellion. Their wings were torn by wrath, their light dimmed by treachery.
It was a fall not just from position, but from presence. Not just from proximity, but from divine fellowship. In an instant, eternity changed—Lucifer became Satan, the Accuser, the Adversary. No longer basking in the warmth of divine light, he was sealed in eternal

separation, cast into darkness, never again to stand in the presence of God's glory.

And thus, the great battle began—an eternal war between light and darkness, holiness and sin, truth and deceit. The righteous King against a wicked enemy. Heaven's perfection against hell's fury.

But this was not the end of God's story. It was the beginning of something new.

At a certain point in eternity, God stirred again with divine intention. He desired something more—something different from the angels who served His throne. Though they were magnificent, their worship, while pure, was instinctual—etched into their being by divine design. But true love, God knew, cannot be compelled. Authentic worship must be chosen.

God longed for intimacy born of freedom.

So, from the formless void, God began a new act of creation. The voice that thundered through the heavens now whispered into the dark—and the darkness obeyed.

"Let there be light."

And light exploded across the void, blazing into the nothingness like a sunrise over an empty world. Galaxies whirled into existence, stars ignited and flung themselves into the night sky like burning jewels. The earth emerged from the deep, swathed in cloud and sea. Mountains thrust toward the heavens, valleys carved themselves into the earth's flesh. Rivers ran like silver veins. Forests rose in emerald splendor. The winds began to sing.

Birds soared on new wings, painting the sky with motion and sound. Beasts thundered across the plains and nestled in the shadows of trees. Fish darted through oceans, glittering like liquid metal beneath the waves. Every leaf, every feather, every scale shimmered with divine intention.

After each act of creation, God looked—and He saw that it was good.

But then came the moment that stilled even the angels.
God said, "Let us make man in our image, after our likeness."

This was no ordinary formation. This was a divine masterpiece, a sacred echo of the Creator Himself. God could have fashioned mankind like the angels—programmed to obey, crafted for service. He could have shaped automations, bound by heavenly instinct. But He didn't.
Instead, He gave humanity something staggering.
He gave us His image.

Not merely in form—but in soul, in imagination, in reason, in will. He placed within us the breath of His own Spirit. And with it, the power to choose.

To choose love.
To choose obedience.
To choose Him.

In giving free will, God took a divine risk. For love that cannot be refused is not love at all. With freedom comes the potential for rebellion—but also the possibility for something greater: true relationship.

There in the garden, in the cool hush of creation's dawn, God formed Adam from the dust. With His own hands, He shaped every line, every sinew. And then—He breathed. The breath of the Almighty filled Adam's lungs, and man became a living soul.
God beheld His creation—and called it good.

He gave Adam dominion over the earth: over sky and sea, bird and beast, every creeping thing that moved upon the land. Authority rippled through Adam's being, a mantle of stewardship placed upon his shoulders. But more than dominion, God gave Adam freedom—the power to choose. And God saw that it was not good for man to be alone.

So, from Adam's side, God fashioned Eve—bone of his bone, flesh of his flesh. She was not a lesser reflection, but an equal partner, radiant and strong, designed for unity. Together, they bore the image of God more completely than either could alone.

Their days were filled with peace, their lives with purpose. They walked with God in the garden, the air alive with glory. And to them, God gave one command:
Do not eat from the tree of the knowledge of good and evil.
For in the day you eat of it, you will surely die.

This was not merely about fruit, it was about trust, about relationship.
About the sacred weight of choice.

To obey, or to defy.
To remain in God's will, or to step outside of it.

By that single command, God affirmed the dignity of humanity. He invited Adam and Eve not into slavery, but into love freely chosen. And in doing so, He gave them the power to shape the course of history—not just for themselves, but for all who would come after.
The future—our future—rested in their hands.

# CHAPTER II - THE ART OF IGNORANCE

I was raised in church.

My earliest memories are painted on a blue stage and purple pews. I remember the soft creak of wooden pews beneath me, the rustle of Bible pages turning in unison, and the sweet, trembling echo of songs that danced through the sanctuary like incense. The pulpit stood like a lighthouse at the front of the room, and I watched my pastor—stoic, passionate, filled with fire—proclaim the Word like thunder wrapped in velvet.

Ministry was in my blood. It coursed through my veins like a divine inheritance. My family was a lineage of preachers, intercessors, and teachers. Our walls were lined with framed photos of revival tents, baptisms in muddy rivers, and the wrinkled hands of saints clasped in prayer. I didn't just go to church—I was encouraged to live it. Scripture wasn't just a book in our home; it was sacred, important, cherished.

By the time I was a teenager, I had read the Bible from Genesis to Revelation more times than I could count. I knew all the stories—the ark that floated on the flood, the sea that split in two, the stone that flew from David's sling and struck down a giant. I knew about Jesus walking on water and Lazarus walking out of the grave. I had all the knowledge, all the exposure, all the right roots.

But no one ever told me that knowing the Scriptures is not the same as knowing the Shepherd.

I thought grace was my birthright. I believed I was spiritually invincible simply because I was raised in a godly house. I wore my faith like a family heirloom, assuming it would always fit. I thought I could live how I wanted, chase what I pleased, and still fall safely into the arms of grace. I thought I would always choose right because everyone expected me to.

But I was wrong.

I went to public school like most kids. I lived in the real world, surrounded by noise, culture, and constant temptation disguised as freedom. And slowly, like a fog creeping in at dawn, a war began to stir inside me. I didn't recognize it at first—it was subtle, patient. But over time, it grew louder, heavier, more relentless.

On one side stood the truth I was raised in—the ancient, unwavering foundation of God's Word. On the other side loomed the allure of the world—its lights, its pleasures, its false promises wrapped in silk and shadows. And right in the middle of it all was me—a teenager with a legacy on his back and a storm in his soul.

If you could see my inner world, you'd see a battlefield. It looked like two armies locked in mortal combat. One, a righteous militia—wearing white uniforms, radiant with the purity of heaven. The other, a dark army—ruthless, eyes burning with lust and rage, bearing the scars of past victories. When I drew close to God, the whitecoats surged forward. But every time I gave in to the desires of the flesh—lust, pride, envy, rebellion—the dark army grew stronger, fed by every compromise.

They were fighting for my soul. And I was the one feeding the war.

No one prepared me for this kind of war. Everyone assumed I was already a soldier because I grew up on a battlefield. But I had never been trained. I had never held the sword for myself. I was alone in the trench, whispering prayers I wasn't sure were reaching heaven, drowning in shame I didn't know how to confess.

Of all the Bible stories etched into my childhood, the one I clung to most was Adam's. I saw myself in him—formed by divine hands, breathed into by the very Spirit of God, placed in a world of beauty and responsibility. Adam was created for greatness, for communion with

God, for dominion. And I believed, with everything in me, that I had a purpose too.

Like Adam, I was raised with everything I needed: guidance, truth, love, legacy.

God had expectations for Adam.
My family had expectations for me.

I loved Adam's origin story—the majesty of Eden, the wonder of walking with God in the cool of the day. It made me feel seen, called, chosen. But for a long time, I skipped over the part where it all fell apart. I ignored the serpent. I brushed past the bite. I clung to the glory of his beginning and avoided the grief of his fall.

Because deep down, I knew I was falling too.

Like Adam, I reached for what looked good but was never meant for me. I tasted sin and expected to stay clean. I chased pleasure and told myself it wasn't poison. I played with fire and convinced myself I wouldn't get burned. I thought I could navigate rebellion and still stay in Eden. But there is always a price for disobedience—and it is always more than you want to pay.

The lie is always the same: "You will not surely die."
But death begins the moment you believe it.

I lost things—peace, innocence, clarity. I started waking up with a weight in my chest that I couldn't name. I smiled in church and crumbled in secret. I lifted my hands in worship and lowered them in shame behind closed doors. I was living a double life, trying to stitch together righteousness and rebellion like oil and water, hoping no one would notice the seams.

And yet, even in the darkest moments—when I felt furthest from God, when I questioned whether I even believed anymore—I could still feel Him. Not in a loud voice or a bolt of lightning. But in a quiet pull. A holy ache. A whisper in my soul saying, "You were made for more."

God wasn't waiting to strike me down. He was waiting to welcome me home.

But first, I had to come to terms with the truth:
Free will is a gift, yes. But it is also a test.
And I had failed.

I had to learn what Adam learned the hard way—that purpose is not protection, and that identity without obedience leads to exile. Eden is not sustained by proximity alone—it's sustained by trust, surrender, and reverence.

And yet—even in exile, God covers.
Even in failure, God speaks.
Even in my fall, He was already planning my redemption.

This was my awakening: not just to the weight of my choices, but to the relentless mercy of a God who doesn't give up on prodigals. A God who speaks even after the fall. A God who walks into the wreckage we've made and whispers, "I still want you."

# CHAPTER III - ACTIONS AND REACTIONS

Growing up, I loved science—especially the discoveries of Sir Isaac Newton. I always found it funny that for over a thousand years, no one had seriously questioned the concept of gravity. Why couldn't we fly? Why didn't we just float off the ground? And the fact that an apple supposedly started it all for Newton? That was mind-blowing to me.

What fascinated me most was how Newton spent his life studying forces—those invisible powers that shape everything around us. As a nerdy kid, I liked to imagine him as some kind of Star Wars geek, trying to understand how to control "the Force." But in reality, he was just observing how God masterfully designed the universe.

Out of all of Newton's laws, the one that has stuck with me the most—and one I still reference as an adult—is this:

For every action, there is an equal and opposite reaction.

What a profound truth. Not just scientifically, but spiritually, emotionally, and morally. Everything we do causes something to happen in return. Every decision carries a consequence—good or bad—and that consequence will influence what happens next.

While I could grasp the gravity of this scientific law, I somehow convinced myself that I was exempt from it when it came to my own life.

My dad would often ask me, after I made a bad decision, "Are you ready for the consequence?" I always said yes.
But in reality, I didn't believe it would actually come. I thought I could outrun the consequences. I thought I was untouchable.

Shortly after turning thirteen, I would engage with one of my peers at school who told me about this website. He spoke to me with animated language and persuasion in his voice, like it was some forbidden secret he had just uncovered—some hidden doorway where you could see girls completely naked. He described it with a mix of excitement and awe, saying you could see what they really looked like beneath their delicate lace blouses and silky satin bras. To him, it was like unlocking a mystery no kid was supposed to know.

That day at school, his words echoed in my mind, stirring something deep and unfamiliar. I found it hard to focus in class. The teachers' voices blurred into the background while my thoughts spun around one question: *What did girls really look like? What was hidden underneath?* The curiosity was overwhelming.

When I got home that evening, the faint sound of the television filled the house as the last rays of sunlight slipped through the window. I headed straight to my room, feeling a strange mix of excitement and nervousness knotting my stomach. The door clicked softly behind me, shutting out the world. I turned the golden lock on the door—as if I could keep my conscience on the other side. I sat down on my bed, the soft fabric of the duvet cool beneath me, and pulled out my tablet.

My fingers hovered over the screen. I felt like I was about to step into the unknown. My breath caught for a moment. Then, with a hesitant but determined tap, I opened the browser. I typed a single word into the search bar: *porn.*

The screen flooded with images I was not prepared for—faces, bodies, moments frozen in time, raw and exposed. I didn't fully understand it, but something stirred inside me. It wasn't shame or fear—it was a new kind of fascination, a deep pull I couldn't resist. I was drawn in, captivated by something I didn't have the tools to process.

That night marked the beginning of a change I didn't see coming. What started as innocent curiosity quickly spiraled into something much darker. I was hooked, deeply and completely, unaware of the battle I was about to face within myself.

For at least six months, I was trapped in a cycle. Day after day, I returned to the screen like a thirsty man to poisoned water, drinking deeply while telling myself it wouldn't kill me. I viewed pornography a minimum of three times a day, sometimes more—consumed by an appetite that grew with every secret indulgence. And still, I felt no conviction. Only a fleeting rush. Momentary pleasure. A counterfeit satisfaction that vanished as quickly as it came.

I told myself no one would ever know. That this hidden life I was building behind closed doors could remain invisible. That the truth would stay buried, locked behind passwords and cleared browsing history. That what I did in secret didn't matter. But it did.
I tried to dig a pit so deep that even God wouldn't peer into it. I tried to veil myself in secrecy, hoping that somehow, I could dodge

divine eyes and escape the truth. I thought I could outrun the consequences.

But consequences always come. And they never knock gently.

Everything changed the day my mother discovered what I had been watching on my device. In that instant, it felt like someone had struck a match in a room drenched in gasoline—the very gasoline I had been carelessly pouring over my soul day after day. And now it was ignited. The fire began to burn.

The shame.
The embarrassment.
The sickening pain of exposure.

It scorched my heart like flame searing through brittle dry wood—fast, merciless, and consuming. Every carefully constructed wall of secrecy collapsed in an instant. There was no hiding anymore. No pretending. What I had hidden in the dark was now out in the blinding, brutal light. And there was no going back.

The reaction—the consequence—had finally arrived.

And I was no longer untouchable.
No longer immune.
I was burning.

The weight of what I had done pressed down on me like a thundercloud collapsing from the sky. The air itself felt heavier, harder to breathe. I was crushed—utterly distraught—shattered in a way I had never felt before. It wasn't just the humiliation of being caught; it was the deep, wrenching ache of knowing I had betrayed more than trust—I had grieved the heart of God.

And in that pain, I felt like Adam—the one I looked up to. But not in his glory, but rather in his fall. After the snake had deceived the woman, after the fruit had been bitten, after the toils and temptations of sin had been released into the world like a tiger from its steel-wire cage—he hid. It was in that moment that I was met with the forced reality that I had been willingly ignorant of. The choice—the bite that cemented death as the narrative of mankind. The disobedience that would send the souls of men into a hell that was created for fallen angels. The knowledge that was never meant to be known.

I realized my nakedness, I had seen my sin, raw and uncut. My heart sank deep into my chest. I was a boy hiding behind the curtains of guilt, praying God wouldn't come looking—but knowing He already had.

This was my moment of reckoning. My reaction. The culmination of every compromise I had made, every corner I had cut, every whisper I had listened to. It all crashed down like a tidal wave—furious and inescapable—dragging me under its weight.

My heart was aflame, not with passion, but with punishment. A wildfire raged inside me, devouring every ounce of peace I once had. Where joy once lived, there was smoke. Where innocence had once played, there was ash. My chest ached with the relentless pounding of guilt, like a war drum beating in my ribs.

Tears blurred my vision as I collapsed onto my knees in the still darkness of my room—the very place where this journey into secret sin had begun. The silence wasn't peace. It was judgment. It pressed against me like a wall, suffocating and thick, filled only by the imagined roar of fire devouring my soul.

I longed for forgiveness, but I felt unworthy of even whispering the request. I saw myself as too far gone—just a pile of burnt wood and broken pieces. I was trapped inside a cage of regret, the bars forged from my own decisions, and the lock sealed with shame.

It was as if the light of God's presence had dimmed. His warmth, once familiar, now felt distant—like standing in the shadow of something I could no longer touch. The fire that consumed me didn't refine me; it left me hollow, emptied, and aching.

I felt small. I felt lost. I felt alone.

And yet—somewhere deep beneath the ash, something flickered. A faint ember that hadn't gone out. A whisper, barely audible: "There is still grace."

The war waged on inside me. The flames of guilt still raged, but there was a spark of hope—a fragile belief that maybe, just maybe, like David, I could fall to my knees, confess it all, and find mercy.

Maybe God wasn't done with me yet.

Even in the ruins.

Even in the fire.

Even here.

# CHAPTER IV - A GALLON OF GASOLINE

"It's not that bad. I'm okay. Everybody does it. I'm not different. It's not hurting me. I can handle it. This is the last time. It's natural. I'm a boy. Society says it's okay."

Those were the lullabies I whispered to my own soul—soft lies to keep my conscience asleep. I told myself that since I was still breathing, since lightning hadn't struck me down, then maybe God didn't really care. Maybe I was still okay.

After a month of swimming in self-pity and denial, I baptized my sin in justification. I called it curiosity. I called it natural. I said I had control. Just a little bit a day. Just enough to take the edge off. Just enough to scratch the itch without letting it bleed. I believed I was the master, not the slave.

But sin never makes room for balance. It is never satisfied with "just a little."

We all have a thing—that "one sin" we can't seem to shake. The one we flirt with like a moth around a flame. Maybe we even hate it, but we keep going back, pulled by its gravity. We cradle it like a wounded animal, but it bites us every time.

It's the sin we pretend helps us. The thing we say is healing us. The one we convince ourselves is part of who we are. And we play with it the way a reckless teenager plays with gasoline—pouring it out, splashing it around, getting it all over us like cologne, and then tucking the matches back into the drawer like everything's fine.

We think if we're careful enough, we won't catch fire.

But the smell lingers. And shame is always watching, holding a lit match between its fingers.

That's what happened to me. I had been playing in a room soaked in gasoline, thinking I was just experimenting, just observing. But when my sin was exposed—when my mother found what I had been hiding—the match dropped.

And the fire came.

Not a fire of cleansing—but a fire of raw, searing shame. A fire that devoured everything I had built in secret. My pride. My sense of control. My excuses. All of it burned.

I tried to hide. Not just from her. I tried to hide from God.

At that moment, I became Adam in the Garden.

The fruit had been eaten. The innocence was gone. And suddenly, I was aware—painfully aware—of my nakedness. My sin. My guilt. I felt the weight of my disobedience like thorns pressed into my skin.

And just like Adam, I ran.

I didn't use fig leaves. I used silence. Isolation. Excuses. I buried myself in distractions and told myself I could fix it. I could manage it. I could clean the gasoline off if I just tried harder.

But it didn't matter how much I scrubbed. The smell was still there. The guilt still clung to my soul like smoke on clothing.

When God called to Adam, "Where are you?" It wasn't because He didn't know. It was because Adam didn't.

That question echoed in my own soul.

Where are you?

Not where you are physically—but spiritually. Where had I gone? Who had I become?

I thought I could manage my sin. I thought I could control it. But the truth was, I had already been overtaken. I was hiding among the trees of my own excuses, hoping God would pass by without noticing the smoke rising from the ruins.

And yet—He came anyway.

God always comes for us. Not to destroy us, but to redeem us. But He doesn't redeem what we're still trying to cover. He redeems what we bring into the light.

That's when I began to realize: in my own strength, I will always choose sin. Over and over again. The flesh doesn't get stronger with time—it gets more deceptive. It learns how to justify, how to dress up rebellion in the costume of curiosity, how to call slavery freedom.

I needed more than discipline. I needed more than willpower. I needed more than guilt.

I needed a Savior.

Because only divine intervention can shatter the grip of sin. Only supernatural strength can lift us out of the dust and cover our shame—not with fig leaves, but with righteousness. Only the blood of Jesus can wash off the gasoline we didn't even know we were soaked in.

Man has tried a thousand ways to fix himself. We see the cycles—addiction, rage, lust, confusion—and we try to medicate the symptoms. We sit in therapy. We take the pills. We finish the programs. We hang our framed diplomas of recovery on the wall. But the fire still smolders inside.

Because healing doesn't come from the outside in.

It comes from the inside out. It begins with surrender. With the confession: "I can't fix myself."

In the Garden, God didn't strike Adam down. He came looking for him. He covered him. But He also showed him that there would be a cost. That sin always brings consequences.

However, He also promised a future—a seed who would crush the serpent's head.

That promise is still true.

In Christ, we're not just covered. We're restored. Reborn. Resurrected.

But only when we stop hiding.
Only when we stop trying to fight fire with flesh.

Only when we bring the gasoline-drenched parts of our lives into the presence of the One who speaks to flames and says, "Be still."

I wish I could say that was the moment everything changed.

That I fell to my knees, weeping for mercy, and walked away forever from the sin that had scorched my soul. I wish I could say the fire was enough—that the shame, the consequence, the pain, snapped me out of it.

But it didn't.

Because the truth is...
I still thought I was stronger than surrender.

Even after the exposure.
Even after the tears.
Even after hearing the crackling roar of my own consequences, I stood back up, brushed the ash off my skin, and walked straight back into the flames. I knew what I was doing.

This time it wasn't innocent curiosity.
This time I wasn't confused.
I was fully aware of what it was, and I did it anyway.

Because pride is blinding. Pride tells you that you're still in control, even when you're completely enslaved. Pride whispers, You can manage this. You're not like everyone else. You'll stop when you want to.
But I couldn't stop.

I went back again—and again—like a dog returning to its vomit. Like Adam not just hiding from God, but stepping further into the shadows of the trees, covering his ears when God called his name.

I told myself I had learned my lesson, but I hadn't.
I told myself I wouldn't go back, but I did.

It was as if something inside me believed that because I had already faced the fire once, I could survive it again. That I could walk barefoot through gasoline and not go up in flames. I had become so familiar with the guilt that I thought I could carry it without consequences. I wore it like a weighted cloak,

dragging behind me, convincing myself that as long as I kept moving forward, I was okay.
But guilt isn't a badge of honor. It's a warning.
And still—I ignored it.

That's the terrifying part about sin: the more you justify it, the less it shocks you. The more you excuse it, the quieter your conscience becomes. I was no longer a boy caught in something shameful—I was a young man growing comfortable in a cage, decorating the walls of my prison and pretending it was home.
And yet, deep down, I knew another fire was coming.

A fire even hotter than before.
A storm darker.
A cost greater.

I knew I couldn't outrun it this time. And still, I didn't stop.
Because surrender felt like weakness.
And I didn't want to be weak.
I didn't want to admit that I couldn't fix myself.

But that's the greatest lie pride ever tells:
That surrender is defeat, when in reality, it's the
doorway to freedom.

I wasn't there yet.
I was still hiding. Still pretending.
Still soaked in gasoline—smelling of
smoke—and daring God to light the match
again.

# CHAPTER V - NOT REFINED, BUT TRANSFORMED

I thought I was Shadrach.
I thought I was Meshach.
I thought I was Abed-Nego.

I imagined that this was my fiery furnace—the trial God had appointed for me. That I was standing faithfully in the midst of the heat, being tested like gold refined in fire. I told myself I was enduring. I told myself I was strong.
But I was wrong.

This wasn't the furnace of trial.
This was the blaze of my own making.

I had poured the gasoline.
I had fed the flame.
I had built the altar and offered myself to a false god.

This fire wasn't holy. It wasn't the testing of the righteous.
It was the punishment of disobedience, the slow burn of compromise, the searing consequence of sin indulged too long.
And yet—
Even in the fire I chose...
Even in the furnace I built with my own two hands...
He was there.
Jesus.

Not standing beside me in honor, like a soldier in battle.
Not clapping me on the back for faithfulness.
But stepping into my mess, into the heat of my rebellion—because He would rather join me in the fire I lit than abandon me to burn alone.

I didn't deserve Him there.
I didn't invite Him.
I didn't even ask for Him.
But He came anyway.

I stood in the middle of my wreckage, the smoke of shame rising thick around me, the smell of scorched identity clinging to my skin, and there He was. Not with arms crossed in judgment. Not with thunder in His voice. But with eyes full of mercy... and scars on His hands. Because that's who He is.

He doesn't just meet the innocent in their trials.
He meets the guilty in their consequences.
He steps into furnaces not just forged by oppressors, but by the sinners themselves.
By me.

I wasn't standing strong like the three in Babylon. I wasn't defying idols. I was bowing. I had compromised. And I didn't come out of that fire without burns.
No—
I came out of the fire with ashes clinging to me—proof of everything I had lost, everything I had burned. But He looked at the ruin and whispered a promise: "I make beauty from ashes."

I came out wounded—heart scorched, soul raw, limping from the weight of my own choices. But He gently reminded me, "By My wounds, you are healed." His blood—red, perfect, and poured out—had already paid for the healing I thought I had to earn.

I told Him my heart was broken, shattered into too many pieces to ever be whole again.

He told me, "Mine broke for you first."

I said, "I ran too far."

He said, "I've been chasing you the whole way."

I was never alone. Not once. Not in the secrecy of sin. Not in the silence of shame. Not even in the fire I built myself. I was never outside of His reach. He was there—waiting. Waiting for me to reach the end of my own strength. Waiting for me to finally step into the fire that burned too hot—so I could see that I couldn't survive it alone.

And it was there—in the flames, in the ruins, in the painful clarity of my own weakness—that I finally made the decision.

No more sitting idly by, halfheartedly listening to the stories I'd grown up hearing. No more pretending the cycle would break on its own. No more convincing myself that "just a little" wouldn't consume me in the end.

I chose Jesus.
Not as a backup plan.
Not as a parachute.
As Lord.

I handed Him everything—my addiction, my pride, my fractured heart, my false strength. I laid them all at the feet of the bruised and bloodied Savior who still looked at me with mercy glossed over His eyes.
I gave Him my life.
Sin no longer had lordship over me. I wasn't its servant anymore. I didn't belong to the shadows—I belonged to the King.

Did the shame and guilt depart from me?
Yes.

Did I feel perfected?
No.

The war wasn't over—but the victory was no longer mine to win.
I had surrendered to the General of Heaven's armies.
And He doesn't lose battles.

Look down the sidewalks. Watch the people pass by.
How many of them are fighting silent battles, trapped in cycles of sin, wearing smiles like armor?
Can you tell?
Can you point them out?

Most of the time, you can't. Because we get good at hiding it.
I was amazing at hiding it.

I knew how to wear the right face, say the right words, blend in just enough to seem fine.
Many didn't know.
Many would have never imagined that I was the one bound in chains so heavy I could barely breathe.
Bound in addiction.
Bound in shame.
Bound in the illusion that I was in control.
But all of that changed on December 7th, 2020.

That was the day everything broke—and everything began.
That was the day I stopped feeding the fire I had built for myself.
That was the day I met freedom.
Most people will never fully know just how much Jesus pulled me out of.
They'll never understand how close I was to the edge—how deeply I had sunk, how exhausted I was from pretending.
But He knew.
And that—that can be your story too.
It doesn't matter what your sin is.

It doesn't matter what altar you've built for your desires.
It doesn't matter how many times you've gone back or how hot the fire has burned around you.
There is another Man in the fire.

He's not watching from a distance.
He's not waiting to condemn you.
He's standing in the heat—hand outstretched, eyes full of mercy—ready to pull you out.

I had fed the war in my mind for too long. I had poured gasoline on my soul and played with flames like they wouldn't burn me.
But then I reached my moment—the breaking point where I had nothing left to give but everything.
And I surrendered it to Him.
And you can too.

Whoever calls on the name of the Lord will be saved.
Anyone caught in a cycle of sin—anyone tired of running—can stop right now and find rest.

But not by fighting harder.
Not by being better.
Only by surrendering.

I wasn't refined by the fire.
I was nearly destroyed by it.
But little did I know, I was about to meet the One
who could transform me.
So maybe today you're standing in your own
fire.
Maybe you're trapped in the same cycle I was,
hoping it won't consume you.

But look up—
You are about to meet the One who walks into
flames to rescue people like us.
The One who doesn't just bring us out—
He makes us new.

# CHAPTER VI - TASTING THE DIRT

"How do I do this?"

That question has lived in my chest more times than I can count

This walk—it feels like a road paved with expectation.

It looks impossible some days.

The standard feels so high.

And honestly? I don't ever want to go back, but forward feels uncertain, unfamiliar, and sometimes unbearably heavy.

I thought about the disciples.

How Jesus called them—pulled them straight out of broken, ordinary lives.

Fishermen. Tax collectors. Zealots.

And they just followed.

No manual. No seminary. Just Him.

How did they do it?

How will I ever figure out how to walk with Him?

Because right now, He's healing wounds I didn't know were still bleeding.

He's stitching together the torn fabric of my heart, piece by piece.
And every day, I feel a little more whole.
But the enemy... he still calls.
Whispers from the shadows, tempting me with familiar pleasures I once thought I couldn't live without.
This decision to follow Jesus—it's not easy.
It's costly.
And it's daily.

There have been many times I've fallen.
Hard. Tasting the dirt, choking on shame, dragging the weight of my past behind me. I'd walk five steps toward Jesus only then to trip over the old sins waiting just around the corner.

But this time... it's different.
Because when I fell, I didn't feel condemnation. I felt His hand.

Gentle. Patient. Steady.
Like a father picking up his child after a bike crash.

Brushing off my scraped knees.
Smiling through the pain.
"Come on," He says. "Let's keep going."

This walk—it feels like getting sea legs on a boat for the first time.
Unsteady, uncertain, swaying with every wave of life.
I feel like the calf of a giraffe—trying to walk on my new, scrawny, legs.
Nobody told me sanctification would be like this.
Nobody told me how much work it would be.
Nobody told me I wouldn't be perfect overnight.
I thought repentance was just a moment—just the altar call.
I didn't know it was a lifestyle. I didn't know I'd have to wake up and choose Jesus again. And again. And again. I thought the enemy would leave me alone once I gave my life to Christ. I thought I'd be immune.
But the voice of temptation? It still whispers. It still knows my name.
And some days, it still sounds like comfort.

No one discipled me.
No one held my hand and walked me into this
new life.
No one explained how messy it would be.
So I cried.
Every night into my pillow, asking Jesus, "Why is
this so hard?"
I pressed my palms to my forehead as the
whispers began again, trying to drown them
out with the truth I was just beginning to learn:
*What I've found in Jesus is worth more than
anything the enemy could offer.*


And maybe your walk looks like mine.
Maybe you're stepping forward in blind
obedience.
Maybe you're still limping, still stumbling, still
unsure how to take the next step.

I know the struggle.
I know the doubt.

I know the face-first falls in the mud and the moments when you swear you'll never get it right. But Jesus never promised it would be easy.

In fact, He said, "If anyone wants to follow Me, let him deny himself, take up his cross, and follow." Denying our nature is the hardest war we'll ever fight. But when we choose Him—when we choose obedience—we reap better consequences. We receive the treasures bought with blood on Calvary's cross.

You're not alone in this journey.
You're not the only one stumbling forward with shaky legs.
This is the real road of discipleship—not always clean, not always strong—but always covered in grace. So keep walking. Even if you're crawling. Even if all you can do today is whisper, "Jesus, help me."
Because He's still the One who lifts the broken, heals the bruised, and walks every step with us—until we stand strong again.

# CHAPTER VII - JUST A CLOSER WALK WITH THEE

I was learning—sometimes clumsily, sometimes painfully—to stand firm, to root myself deeply in God's Word. Like Peter, who stumbled repeatedly yet never stopped following Jesus, I was trying to obey even when I was unsure, even when I faltered. Peter, who boldly declared he would never deny Jesus, ended up denying Him three times before the rooster crowed. Yet, despite those failures, Jesus restored him, called him back, and entrusted him with leading the early church. His story gave me hope—that even in my mess-ups, Jesus would not give up on me.

I discovered that my help came not from my own strength, but from Him alone. Every step I took felt weighted with significance. Every choice mattered. It was overwhelming—sometimes even frightening—to realize how much my future hinged on the small, daily decisions I made.

When I turned fourteen, something shifted. The battle wasn't just between light and darkness anymore. I wasn't merely running away from the flames that had once burned me. Instead, I was running toward the Savior, chasing after Him with all my heart. Was it easy? Far from it.

But I clung to a song that became my anthem, my prayer:
*"Just a closer walk with Thee,*
*Grant it, Jesus, is my plea,*
*Daily walking close to Thee,*
*Let it be, dear Lord, let it be."*
How was I supposed to make it if I wasn't pursuing Him? If I wasn't striving to obey? In those moments, I felt the calling of ministry stirring within me—a path both holy and terrifying, like standing at the edge of a dark forest, unsure of the way forward. But I held onto the hope that if I just walked closer with Jesus, if

I chose Him over the tempting whispers that threatened to pull me back, maybe, just maybe, I could make it.

Peter's journey mirrored this tension. He was a fisherman, rough around the edges, impulsive, and often unsure, yet Jesus called him to leave everything behind and follow. Peter walked on water—until doubt pulled him under. He boldly spoke up, only to be silenced by fear. He was human, full of flaws, yet deeply loved and chosen by Jesus.

Isn't that how it is for all of us? We barely manage to get through each day by Christ alone. Who else can carry the weight of our battles? Who else can steady our trembling steps? Is He truly enough?

Like many, I walked this path without a guide—no mentor, no hand to hold. Though Christ calls us all to disciple one another, to walk together in faith, I learned mostly on my own. By the Man Himself. That meant learning the hard way, not the easy way.

I had to discern truth from lies, good choices from bad. I had tasted the bitter fruit of sin, seen the swift consequences that follow every wrong decision. I had already given the enemy consent to light the match and burn me once. But on this new walk with Christ, I was determined not to turn back.

Now, stepping forward into the ministry, the path seemed even more daunting. I knew I needed wisdom to make better choices—not to stumble into old patterns of destruction, but to burn with a different fire. No longer a fire that destroys, but the holy fire of God, refining and empowering me to live for Him.

Peter's story is a powerful reminder that faith is not perfection—it's persistence. After his denial, Jesus didn't reject Peter. Instead, He sought him out on the shore, asked him three times if he loved Him, and commissioned him to feed His sheep. That restoration gave Peter a new purpose and strength to walk boldly forward, despite his past failures.

Like Peter, we are not perfect. We don't have all the answers. But we must choose to follow, to surrender, to trust that the same grace that restored Peter will transform us too.

# CHAPTER VIII - A SECOND FLAME

Every Sunday, I walked into church expecting routine—but routine was not what met me. Something had begun to change. The words of the preacher no longer drifted past me like a gentle breeze; they hit with the force of a storm. My ears, once dulled by distraction, were now tuned to something deeper—something divine. His voice carried weight, urgency, as though eternity were pressing through every syllable. I sat still, breath held, heart pounding, when the altar calls rang out. The moment the preacher cried for the fire of God to fall, I felt a thrill in my bones—electric, undeniable.

It was no longer just a moment in the service. It was the very moment I lived for.

This fire—this Holy Fire—was unlike anything I'd ever known. It wasn't just thrilling; it was alive. It stirred something ancient in me, something eternal. I had known fire before—the other fire, the one that lured with pleasure and left only ruin. I had once opened the door to it, allowed it to consume parts of me that were never meant to burn. I let it scar my flesh and sear my soul, and I bore its marks like chains. But this—this fire—was different. It didn't scorch me into shame. It awakened me. It made me hungry. I began to pray with desperation, pleading not for blessings or breakthroughs, but for the Holy Spirit to come and ignite me from within. I begged for that fire to enter the deepest parts of me and set my heart ablaze, not with lust or pride, but with purpose.

I had given myself to the first flame, and it left me hollow. Now I was giving myself to the second flame—the flame of the Spirit—and it was making me whole. It didn't just touch me; it claimed me. It branded me as holy, set apart, no longer belonging to this world or its twisted fires. This new flame gave me courage. It gave me a voice. It made me rise to proclaim freedom to the captives, to shout into the darkness with a boldness I never knew I had. I had made a choice—and this time, it was not a choice for pleasure, but for power. Not for ease, but for eternal fire.

Life—this strange, brutal, beautiful life—offers us two flames. The fire of sin, and the fire of God. Both flicker with allure. Both whisper promises. Sin's fire is seductive. It masks its venom in delight. It wraps itself around your senses, your desires, feeding your hunger with poisoned sweets. But once the thrill fades, it leaves behind its true gift—shame. Emptiness. A gnawing ache that pleasure cannot soothe. That fire takes, and takes, and takes—until there's nothing left.

But the fire of God? Oh, the Holy Fire—it's not so subtle. It doesn't seduce; it calls. It calls you to die, so you can live. It burns away the rot of this world: the bitterness, the jealousy, the secret sins. It strips you down, but not to shame you—to purify you. To make you gold. It doesn't whisper—it roars. It roars with holiness, with presence, with power. And if you dare to let it in, if you dare to open yourself wide to it, it will consume you—but not destroy you. It will make you new.

Yet even this fire must be tended. It will not burn forever on neglect. If you do not pour oil into the lamp, the flame will wither. It demands a sacrifice—not once, but daily. You must climb upon the altar again and again and say, "Here I am. Burn in me." That is the life of a living sacrifice. That is the call. Never step down. Never walk away. Choose the fire, always the fire.

What is this fire that I speak of? It is judgment. It is the holy, terrifying opposition of God to all sin. In His fire, no impurity survives. It is refinement, like gold in the crucible, the heat revealing what must be removed. It is presence—manifest, undeniable. Not always warm and comforting. Sometimes it is overwhelming. Sometimes it drives you to your knees, trembling beneath glory too heavy to bear.

But it is also empowerment. The fire of God ignites the voice of the prophet, the courage of the martyr, the faith of the servant. It is the same fire that led Israel through the wilderness, a pillar of flame in the blackest night, showing the path when all seemed lost. It is the fire that changes everything it touches. It reduces the old to ash. It reveals the pure. It makes the broken new.

And in the days of old, when a man brought his sacrifice to the altar, it was fire from heaven that consumed it. That fire was God's answer. That fire said, "I accept." So now I live my life on the altar, waiting for that fire—calling for it. I was not made to sit in the shadows. I was not made to flicker and fade. I was created to burn. To blaze with His glory, until the world sees not me, but the One who lit the flame. This same calling—this same commandment, is as much for you as it is for me.

# CHAPTER IX - SHADOWED CONVERSATIONS

Still, the voices slithered from the shadows, low and venomous. "How is he doing this?" one hissed. "Where has he gone?" another whispered with a snarl. "He can't ignore me." "He's still mine." Their words wrapped around my thoughts like smoke, thick and suffocating. I could feel the darkness thinking—plotting—scrambling to understand how I had slipped through their grasp. The enemy was not silent; he was stirred. I could hear the demons muttering in hushed, frantic tones—shame and guilt conspiring like old lovers, desperate to win me back. They were strategizing, weaving lies, reaching into my memories to find something—anything—that would drag me back into the pit. They weren't done with me. They were still fighting for me.

But I kept running—chasing after the fire.

Not just any fire—that fire. Righteous. Holy. The fire that does not burn to destroy, but to make holy ground for ordinary men. I wanted it more than I had ever wanted anything in my life. I wanted it to consume me, to set every inch of me ablaze until there was nothing left of the old me to fight for. I didn't want to just feel it. I wanted to become it. A living flame in the hands of God.

Somewhere deep in my soul, I believed—maybe even hoped—that if God would only set me fully ablaze, if He would use me in power for His glory, then the voices in the dark would finally fall silent. That the whispers would melt away in the heat of His presence. That the shame would lose its grip. That the demons would flee, scorched by the fire that now burned in me.

I wasn't running to escape the darkness anymore. I was running because I had seen a light—and now, I wanted to be that light.

It always came back to choices. No matter how far I ran, how deeply I prayed, how loudly I worshiped—it circled back to that one truth. I had to choose. Daily. Hourly. Moment by moment. The war wasn't just in the heavens—it was in me, between spirit and flesh, desire and discipline, truth and temptation.

I found myself constantly counting the cost, tracing every decision down to its possible end. Weighing the invisible consequences that felt more real than anything I could touch. I was learning—slowly, painfully—how to choose Jesus. Not just in word, not just when the music swelled or the altar called, but in the quiet moments, in the solitude, in the tension. I was choosing Him in the absence of reward, in the silence that followed obedience.

Because the blessings hadn't come yet.

I was in pursuit of Him, and I believed with everything in me that He was worth it—but my eyes hadn't yet seen the fruit of that choice. No breakthroughs, no open doors, no divine rewards neatly packaged and delivered. Just obedience. Just faith. Just the flame.

But something in me knew—this was where it mattered most. Choosing Him not for what He could give, but for who He was. Trusting that the blessings would come, even if I couldn't yet trace their shape on the horizon. Choosing to chase the fire, even when it didn't light my path, only burned within my chest.

But just like my bad choices, the consequences always came. They are never delayed forever. Sin was seductive in the moment, but its shadow always arrived—sometimes quick, sometimes slow, but always certain. They always arrive. And in that same truth, I began to find hope.

Because if that was true for my bad choices, then it must also be true for the good ones. If pain followed rebellion, then surely peace would follow obedience. If sin bore fruit in suffering, then righteousness must bear fruit in glory—even if I hadn't seen it yet.

I was learning to believe that the consequences of choosing Jesus would come too. They might not rush in with fireworks or fanfare, but they were coming—quiet, steady, certain. Healing would come. Restoration would come. Joy, purpose, power—they would all come in their time. My obedience was not in vain. My pursuit was not empty.

The same law that governed the bitter harvest of my failures was now working in my favor. Seed by seed, step by step, I was sowing into something eternal. And I knew—the fire was working. Even if I couldn't yet see it, even if the shadows still whispered, the consequences of faithfulness were already on their way.

# CHAPTER X - REAPING MY HARVEST

I remember the exact moment the light switched on in my spirit. It wasn't just another prayer, another whisper into the heavens. It was revelation. I had been begging God for fire—pleading, weeping, crying out in desperation—but something shifted. I realized I had to contend for it. Not just wait. Not just wish. But stand on His Word and believe.

Scripture says, "Ask, and it shall be given you; seek, and ye shall find; knock, and it shall be opened unto you." I had asked, I had sought, but this was the moment I started standing—rooted in promise, firm in faith. The throne room of heaven doesn't ignore a heart that contends. The ears of the Almighty are tuned to the cry of the persistent.

And then—it came.

Not in a church service. Not through the hands of a preacher or a fiery altar call. I had expected the dramatic: a laying on of hands, oil anointing my forehead, people shouting and praising in crescendo. I thought the fire had to come with spectacle. But God, in His mercy, chose something better.

I was alone. Sick. Quarantined with the coronavirus. No audience, no stage—just me, my Bible, and my broken expectancy. And it was there, in the silence of my bedroom, that heaven cracked open.

The fire of the Holy Spirit descended—not metaphorically, but tangibly. I felt my chest ignite, not with fever but with a holy blaze. My tongue trembled, then loosened with a language I had never learned. My eyes wept without end. My breath was taken, yet I could breathe just fine. It wasn't mine anymore—it was His.

This must have been what the prophets of old felt. When the Spirit of the Lord would come upon them like a rushing wind—uninvited yet always welcomed. Terrifying and yet gloriously right. I was undone. I was consumed. I was changed.

This wasn't a gift man could give me. This was between me and my Lord. Like the day of Pentecost, when the fire sat upon each of the disciples, the flame rested on me—not borrowed fire, not secondhand anointing. My encounter. My moment.

And then I heard Him—clear as thunder in my soul:
"Share of this goodness. Tell them about Me."

It jolted me. The Voice. I couldn't disobey. Shaking, still weeping, I grabbed my phone, opened Facebook, and started a live video right there on my bedroom floor. I spoke with trembling lips, pouring out praises, sharing the goodness of God, declaring that what I had found could belong to anyone. This fire could dwell in your temple, too.

No one was watching. The live feed was empty. A small sting of discouragement touched me—but only for a moment. I had obeyed. That was enough. I turned off the camera, laid the phone down, and returned to the fire. I wanted more—not more viewers, not more affirmation—just more of Him.

And this, I believe, is the essence of the fire of God. Not theatrics. Not hype. Not borrowed heat. But a personal, holy, consuming, life-altering presence. It burns away the chaff. It silences the doubt. It scars you in the best way—leaving marks of glory and not shame.

I was dead. Not in body, but in spirit—burnt out by sin, choked by smoke, buried in ashes. I had fed the wrong fire for too long, the kind that promises warmth but leaves you scorched. The world's fire had scarred me, drained me, nearly consumed me. But then—His fire came.
Not a fire of destruction, but of revival. It found me in my weakness, in my sickness, in my bedroom when no one was watching. It didn't

need a preacher, a stage, or a performance. It was just me, the Word, and the Spirit of God. And when it fell, I knew—I had come alive again.

This fire didn't just warm me. It changed me. It purified what was broken, ignited what was cold, and stirred a boldness in me I never knew I had. I had once consented to be burned by sin. Now, I had chosen to burn for Him.

And I couldn't keep it to myself.

This wasn't just for me. The fire was meant to spread. Jesus said we are the light of the world—not hidden, but burning on display. This fire is revival, and it's not meant to stay in one heart. It's meant to move.

I was dead.
But now I burn.
And I will carry this fire wherever He leads me—
Until the world is set ablaze.

You may be dead—spiritually dry, burnt out, lying still like the underbrush on a forest floor, waiting for breath to return. Maybe you've been crying into your pillow, pleading with God to pour out His fire. Maybe you're done with the first flame—the one that left you in pain—and you're finally ready for the fire that revives, refines, and restores.

You've been praying. Days. Months. Maybe years. Going from church to church, conference to conference, sitting beneath every anointed voice you could find, hoping that this would be the moment. That this preacher, this worship set, this altar call, would be the one to light the match.

But hear me—that's not the story.

You don't need another performance. You don't need another man to lay hands on you. What you need is to stand on the Word.
Hold to the promise:

"Ask, and it will be given to you; seek, and you will find; knock, and it will be opened to you." (Matthew 7:7)

If you ask—truly ask—He will answer. If you stay on the altar—if you remain surrendered—then when the wildfire of God's Spirit moves through the land, it will find you ready. It will consume your dead places and raise you in holy flame.

This could be your story.
Revival is real.
And it starts with a single spark of surrender.

# CHAPTER XI - BRANDED

It was later that same day—after the medicine, after the weeping, after the nap that felt more like collapse than rest—that I reached for my phone. Just curiosity, that's all. A glance to see if anyone had watched the video. Maybe one or two. Maybe five.

But there it was.

Fifty. Two hundred thirty. Six hundred seventy-eight. Nine hundred eighty-two. One thousand, two-hundred eighty.

The numbers climbed until they stopped at 1,270 views. Me, a teenager in his bedroom, sick, sweating, crying, and praying—reaching over a thousand souls.

I didn't even know that many people.

How could this one, broken, little video travel that far?How could a kid like me reach that many?

And then I heard it—His voice again—clearer this time.

"This is who you are. You will preach of My goodness."

It wasn't a suggestion. It was a commissioning.

And from that moment, my ministry was born.

It didn't come with blinding lights or a booming voice on a dusty road like Saul of Tarsus. I wasn't a Lester Sumrall or a Leonard Ravenhill. No one threw me onto a platform. I wasn't in a church sanctuary. I was in my room, alone—but not really alone.

It happened with Him.

But the fire that ignites a calling also demands a choice.

Would I run with this fire—or would I run from it?

I wish I could say I immediately leapt at the call, that I sprinted forward like Isaiah saying, "Here I am, Lord, send me." But the truth is, I hesitated. I wrestled. For months I posted online, teaching what little I knew of the Word, letting others share what God was placing on their hearts. But ministry? Full-time? That wasn't the life I imagined.

I had dreams. Ambitions. I wanted to be a forensic scientist, a coroner, a criminal profiler. I loved the world of psychology and pathology. Where was the pulpit in that?

Ministry was my Nineveh—and like Jonah, I ran. My ambitions became the fish that swallowed me. I tried to swim against the current of His call.

But God is patient. He redirected me, again and again, back to Him.

Eventually, after all the tossing, after the sleepless nights and wrestling in prayer, I surrendered. I chose Him—not halfway, but with everything I had. College didn't matter. Careers didn't matter. He called, and I said yes.

Did the surrender come easy? No. It came with a thousand tiny deaths. Like Paul said in 1 Corinthians, "I die daily." I had to crucify my own ambitions. I had to lay them on the altar.
But it also came with fire.
Fire that refines. Fire that purifies. Fire that consumes the old and births the new.

Isaiah saw this kind of fire too. In the year King Uzziah died, the prophet saw the Lord high and lifted up. Seraphim took a coal from the altar and touched his lips. It burned, but it also cleansed. "Your guilt is taken away and your sin atoned for" (Isaiah 6:7). Only then did Isaiah hear the call: "Whom shall I send?" And he answered, "Here I am. Send me."

Like Isaiah, I had to be cleansed before I could be commissioned.
Like Jonah, I had to stop running before I could walk in obedience.
Like Paul, I had to die to myself before I could live for Him.

I chose it. I consented to a life marked not by the first flame of destruction, but by the second flame—the one that consecrates and commissions, that burns but does not consume.
The fire fell. The calling came. And from that moment on, there was no turning back. I was branded by fire.

# CHAPTER XII - A FAMILIAR VOICE

But what happened to the enemy? Did he disappear?

What became of all the schemes he plotted, the groanings and snarls of his legions of demons? What happened to shame, temptation, guilt, and embarrassment? Did they all simply die, vanish into thin air, never to be seen again?

I wish I could say that was the case.

It was just when I started gaining momentum, just when I began to run with the new calling God had placed on my life, that a familiar voice crept back in—whispering into my ear, appealing to the old wounds, the old desires, the very things that once burned me. It didn't come through fire or thunder. It came softly, subtly, wearing a face I longed for: relationship.

I had always wanted a wife and children. Even as a young man, I knew that desire was placed in me by God, and I trusted He would provide. But then a certain girl came along. She was beautiful—yes—but even more than that, she was endearing. She wasn't the kind of person who seemed like trouble. She wasn't wild or dangerous; she didn't even know she was being used as a distraction. She was innocent, but when I tethered myself to her, it weighed me down. I knew the heaviness on my spirit wasn't from God.

Like David standing on the rooftop, looking out over Jerusalem only to have his eyes settle on Bathsheba, I was caught off guard by something that felt natural—but was deeply dangerous. David, the man after God's own heart, still fell. He still gave in to desire. And when the weight of his sin finally caught up with him, he cried out to God not for success, not even for rescue—but for relationship. "Cast me not away from Your presence, and take not Your Holy Spirit from me." David didn't fear punishment as much as he feared distance from God. I began to understand that cry.

I started noticing the toll—spiritually, emotionally. I wasn't running like I used to. The fire still burned in me, but it wasn't as bright, not as hot. The anointing didn't flow the way it once had. The favor didn't feel the same. Somewhere, I had compromised. And where was it? In a relationship God never called me to. I had taken my eyes off the flame.

That old, familiar voice began to speak louder again—whispers of doubt, failure, condemnation. And then I fell. Not like I had fallen before. This fall was heavier. It stuck. I had returned to the very chains God had once shattered off my life.

I don't hear many preachers talk about that. The backsliding, falling again. We talk about victories, about boldness, about strength—but what about the wrestling? What about the times when you know better, yet still falter? Where are the sermons about those days?

The truth is, every man of God has a weakness. And for some of us, the enemy keeps trying that same door again and again, hoping one day we'll forget to lock it. Temptation returns. It always does. The battle never ends on this side of glory. But I've learned that even when we fall, even when we stumble into sin again, God's voice still speaks. And it speaks a better word.

What we have in Jesus is worth getting back up for. His grace is worth contending for. I realized I had to stand up again. I had to pray like David, not for comfort or restoration of favor—but, "Lord, do not take Your Spirit from me." I asked Him to remove anything in my life that wasn't helping me grow, anything that dulled the fire. And little by little, He did. The breakup hit hard. Even though deep down I knew the relationship wasn't right, it still hurt to let go. It wasn't a dramatic ending — no shouting, no blame —

just a quiet realization that I had to walk away from something I never should have stepped into. I had invested so much of myself into building a future with her, even when the foundation was cracked from the start. And when it all came down, it felt like I was left standing in the rubble, trying to figure out who I was without her.

There was this emptiness she left behind — not just the absence of her, but of everything I had attached to the idea of us. The comfort, the distraction, the false sense of security. It was all gone, and I had to trust that God could fill the spaces she no longer occupied — not with another person, not with noise, but with something real.

It wasn't easy. Healing never is. But piece by piece, I started to feel myself come back. Stronger this time. Clearer. I learned that letting go of what's wrong can be just as important as holding on to what's right. And sometimes, the hardest goodbyes are the ones that bring you back to yourself.

After the testing and the changing, after the refocusing and the long nights of being redirected back to where I belonged, the enemy didn't disappear. He didn't pack up and leave just because I was on the right track. No, he lingered. He watched. He waited for moments of weakness, for cracks in the armor. He still whispered the same old lies, still tried to resurrect the shame I had buried, still showed up in the quiet moments when I was alone with my thoughts. But something had changed — not in him, but in me.

The voice of God was louder now. Steadier. It wasn't just a voice I listened for in crisis; it became the soundtrack of my every day. His Word began to shape how I saw myself — not as someone barely hanging on, but as someone chosen, someone equipped, someone called. His promises became my anchors, not just verses I quoted but truths I lived. His presence reminded me that I wasn't walking alone anymore.

Where shame tried to drag me down, love lifted me. And when I faltered, God didn't turn away — He called me back, every time, with grace that refused to let go. I realized that the battle wasn't about silence or escape; it was about which voice I chose to believe. And every day, I chose the One who called me son.

I had tasted the fire. I had known the presence of the Lord. And I would do anything to stay near it. Even after the fall, I found revival again—not because I was strong, but because God was faithful. Just like He was with David.

# CHAPTER XIII - THE SOIL OF SURRENDER

I continued stronger—stronger than I had ever been before. As I pressed forward, running the race set before me, I began to witness something beautiful: the blessings of God began to overtake me. They followed me like the trailing light behind a torch in the dark, illuminating the path, marking my journey with signs of His favor. But as I looked at these blessings, I found myself asking a sobering question: Why?

Was it because I was good? Absolutely not. Was it because I was righteous, a man of God with some special title or badge of honor? No. The truth was more humbling than that. These blessings didn't follow me because of who I was, but because of what I chose to do. I sowed. I sowed not into the soil of my own ambition, not into the world's empty promises, but into the fertile ground of Jesus Christ.

There is a divine principle that stretches across the whole Word of God like a golden thread—the law of seedtime and harvest. "Be not deceived, God is not mocked: for whatsoever a man soweth, that shall he also reap." I used to wonder how to reap good things. I wanted to see miracles, to witness healing, to experience the kind of freedom that breaks chains and silences demons. But I didn't know where to sow. I didn't know what good soil looked like.

Now I do.

This life I'm building with Jesus—it has revealed itself as soil rich with grace, watered by mercy, and warmed by the radiant love of the Son. Everything planted here grows. It may not always sprout immediately, but it always bears fruit. You may be reading this in a storm, knee-deep in struggle, and wondering why nothing is going your way. Let me ask you: When was the last time you sowed a seed? Not into your own comfort or control, but into the soil of God's goodness?

When was the last time you said, "Lord, I trust You with this"? Your time. Your tears. Your talents. Your treasure. When was the last time you offered them up and trusted God to multiply them? Because He will. That's His nature. He is the Lord of the harvest. And whatever you sow into His soil, He will return to you pressed down, shaken together, and running over.
You weren't made for squalor. You were made for overflow.

But hear me: God will not force overflow on anyone. You must choose Him. You must plant. You must water in prayer, and wait in faith. You are the one who determines where your seed goes, which direction your life turns, what words your tongue speaks, what paths your feet walk. You were made with free will, and God honors that. Jesus is Lord, yes—but He does not drive; He leads. And you must choose to follow.

He is the only one who can rewrite your story. He is the only one who can redeem what sin has ruined. He alone can speak to dead places and bring them to life again. And when you choose Him—when you choose to pour your life into His hands—He will pour His Spirit into your soul until you overflow with purpose, joy, and peace.

And this brings us to the cross.

All of this—every blessing, every promise, every miracle, every answered prayer—is not because of your effort or your morality. It was purchased. And the currency was the blood of a sinless Savior. On a lonely hill called Golgotha, Jesus—the Lamb of God without blemish or spot—was lifted high on a Roman cross. His hands were pierced, not just by nails, but by the weight of humanity's guilt. His back was torn open by lashes that should have been ours. His brow was crowned with thorns, mockery pressed into majesty.

He was betrayed, abandoned, and condemned. Spat upon by those He came to save. Crucified between criminals as if He were one of them. The sky turned black. The earth quaked. The veil tore. And there, with His final breath, He cried out, "It is finished." Not defeated—but victorious. He didn't say "I am finished," but "It is finished." The price of your redemption, the penalty of your sin, the consequence of your shame—it was all paid in full.

This is not just history—it is your inheritance.

We are not asking Him to do something new; we are asking to step into what has already been done. We are reaching out to claim the reward of His suffering. You and I, we now have access to what His blood purchased. And His blood is more precious than silver or gold. It speaks a better word.

So choose Him. Sow into Him. And let the fire of His love consume you, not for a moment, but for a lifetime. For this Jesus—crucified, resurrected, glorified—is not just a chapter in your life. He is the Author. And He's still writing.

# CHAPTER XIV - GAINING MOMENTUM

It had been months since I had fallen—since the weight of shame and compromise had wrapped itself around my ankles and slowed my pace. But in that wilderness, I returned to the basics. I began to rebuild the altar. Quiet mornings spent in the Word. Whispered prayers in my room when no one else was listening. No demands, no expectations—just pursuit. I wasn't chasing a blessing anymore. I was chasing Jesus.

I began to understand what it meant to seek His face, not His hand. I started to believe that maybe this was the simple life of a Christian: to know God, to walk with Him daily, and to receive the miracles and breakthroughs on occasion—as rare, sweet outpourings of grace. I was content with that.

But then, something shifted. It was as if the windows of heaven were flung open, and instead of drops, there came a downpour—blessings that couldn't be contained. The Lord began to restore what the enemy had tried to destroy.

I had recently left a church where I had been deeply mistreated—where I was seen not as a son of God but as a tool to be manipulated. My identity had been pushed aside in favor of performance. My free will was ignored and my convictions were disrespected. But God used even that betrayal to draw me deeper into His presence. What the enemy meant for evil, God intended for good.

Then came the calling. Like the still, small voice that spoke to Elijah on the mountain, God whispered clarity and direction. He led me to a specific ministry school—one I had never considered before, but one where I would be shaped, equipped, and launched. I applied, prayed, and waited. And in a moment of divine favor, I was accepted. Doors opened that no man could shut.

A month before the program began, the school added us all into a Facebook group to meet one another. That's where I saw her. Not the distraction or counterfeit I had encountered before. She didn't pull me away from God; she ran with me toward Him. She wasn't lukewarm or half-committed. She had fire in her eyes for Jesus. As I pursued her, I never lost sight of Christ—and I knew deep in my spirit, this was part of the blessing. The promise was fulfilled, the favor manifested.

I started ministry school and was imparted with some of the most profound teachings of my life. I didn't just learn *about* the call—I felt it deepen. My understanding expanded. My spiritual senses sharpened. And the blessings? They became regular. Consistent. Day after day, I watched the faithfulness of God unfold like a scroll before me.

I often found myself reflecting on the early days—those long, quiet nights when I cried into my pillow wondering, "Will it ever get better? Will the fire ever come back?" Now, not only had the fire returned, but it burned hotter, brighter, and stronger than ever before.

It felt like the war in my mind had shifted.

For years, it was a battlefield soaked in blood—mine. Every thought was a swinging sword, every doubt a fiery arrow. The enemy, once loud and unrelenting, roared like a lion, stalking the borders of my soul. He prowled in the shadows, knowing every weakness, speaking in the familiar voice of guilt, shame, and regret. He was strategic, relentless—planting lies like landmines, waiting for the perfect moment to strike.

But something began to change.

The whispers of Heaven grew louder than the howls of hell. Scripture became my sword, and prayer my shield. Day by day, inch by inch, the white-robed army of Heaven pressed forward into the dark places of my heart. Angels of the

Most High marched in rhythm to the Word of the Lord, and the presence of the Holy Spirit swept like a cleansing wind through the chambers of my mind.

The darkness began to retreat.

Where once stood fortresses of fear, faith now built towers of strength. The enemy's strongholds—those mental patterns, temptations, and lies—crumbled beneath the weight of truth. The Word of God, alive and active, sharper than any two-edged sword, cut through the lies that had once kept me captive.

It was like watching a defeated army flee the battlefield, gasping for air, desperate to find a foothold in a land no longer theirs. They scrambled through the ashes of what used to be my past, but found no ground to stand on—because that ground now belonged to the Lord. It had been bought with blood. Consecrated. Claimed.

The enemy's voice—once a thunderclap in my soul—was now a dying whisper, barely audible beneath the roar of freedom. I could feel it: peace settling in like a banner over my life. "Jehovah Nissi"—The Lord is my banner. His presence no longer visited; it dwelt.

The war had not vanished, but the tide had turned.

The battlefield was still scorched from years of conflict, but now it bore fruit. What once was trampled and war-torn was now a vineyard being tended by the hand of God. And though the enemy still lurked on the fringes, he no longer ruled the terrain. The King had taken the throne in my heart, and every step I took was under His command.

Victory, I realized, doesn't always look like the absence of battle—it looks like knowing who already won it.

It had been three, maybe four years since I had made the decision to pursue the God who had never stopped pursuing me—and I was finally seeing the harvest.

I would go on to marry that girl. She became not only my wife but my partner in purpose, a co-laborer in the harvest field, and my best friend. The friendships I formed at that school were more than seasonal—they were spiritual iron that sharpened me. God had not only poured out blessing but had built a foundation for the future.

And it wasn't because I was worthy. It wasn't because I had earned anything. But the Word declares a spiritual law and I had made the decision to sow into the Spirit. I planted seeds of obedience, faith, purity, and surrender—and the fruits of righteousness were multiplied in my life. I don't just serve the God of increase, but the God of multiplication.

Good choices. Godly soil. Consistent sowing.
And the harvest was rich.

This is the Kingdom. Not a life of perfection, but a life of pursuit. Not a life without pain, but a life with purpose. When you choose Jesus over compromise, holiness over hype, and the altar over applause, the blessings will follow—not always instantly, not always in the form you expect—but always in the form you need.

The fire comes. The rain comes. And the Father, in His goodness, never fails to bring increase to the seeds sown in faith.
Maybe you're reading this right now, and you've been sowing faithfully for years. You've cried out in prayer, laid seeds of obedience, tears, and sacrifice into the ground again and again. You've waited, watched, and hoped — but still, the harvest hasn't come. The breakthrough you've believed for feels delayed. The fruit seems hidden beneath hard soil.

Let me encourage you: God is still working. He has never stopped working for you. Even when Heaven seems silent, your prayers are not forgotten. The Father is not idle — He is weaving things together beneath the surface, cultivating a harvest in hidden places. Just because you haven't seen the rain doesn't mean the clouds aren't gathering.

But there is something critical in these seasons of waiting: instead of asking, "God, why haven't You?", begin to ask, "God, what else can I surrender?"

How much deeper can your surrender go? How many more minutes can you spend at the altar, not to beg for answers, but to simply be with Him? Sometimes we are asking for the fruit while still holding onto things that keep us from receiving it. We're praying for increase, while clinging to the very things that choke the soil. This is the refining fire. This is the threshing floor. This is where you shift your prayers from asking for provision to asking for Presence. You stop pleading for blessing and begin crying out for the Blesser.

Jesus said, "Seek first the Kingdom of God and His righteousness, and all these things will be added to you." He is not just the Giver — He is the gift. When you shift your focus from the fruit to the Vine, from the blessing to the Builder, you begin to discover the joy of simply knowing Him. He said in John 15, "I am the true vine, and My Father is the vinedresser... Abide in Me, and I in you. As the branch cannot bear fruit of itself unless it abides in the vine, neither can you, unless you abide in Me." This is the secret to fruitfulness — not striving, but staying; not producing, but abiding.

It is only in remaining connected to Christ — rooted in His Word, yielded in prayer, anchored in obedience — that we begin to bear fruit that lasts. The branch has no life apart from the Vine. We can build platforms, accumulate possessions, and chase dreams, but if we are not drawing from the life source of Christ, that fruit will rot before it ripens. The world chases productivity; the Kingdom calls us to proximity. He never asked us to perform — He asked us to remain.

Remaining close to Jesus doesn't just change your outcomes, it transforms your heart. It recalibrates your desires. It silences the noise and awakens the Spirit within. You begin to crave what pleases Him. You begin to reflect the nature of the One you're near. And the fruit you bear — peace, love, joy, patience, self-control — doesn't come from effort, but from intimacy. You don't have to force a branch to bear fruit when it's properly attached to the Vine.

So keep yourself close. Cling to Him when you don't see results. Cling to Him when the blessings delay. Let your life be marked not by what you accomplish for Him, but how faithfully you remain in Him. Because in the end, fruit is not the goal — Jesus is. And He is enough.

This is the key: fruit grows where intimacy is rooted.

So don't despise the waiting. Don't curse the quiet seasons. Instead, crawl deeper into the heart of God. Turn your altar into a dwelling place. Keep your seed in the soil. Water it with worship. Protect it with faith. And trust — trust with all your heart — that the harvest is coming. Because in His timing, and in His way, it always does.

And when that harvest finally comes — when you begin to see the fruit of years of prayer, surrender, and silent obedience — let your first response be reverence. Not pride, not entitlement, but awe. The kind of awe that brings you to your knees in quiet gratitude, trembling not at what *you* have accomplished, but at the mercy of a God who saw your secret faith and honored it. It is here, in the place where blessing meets brokenness, where favor collides with faith, that we learn to fear the Lord rightly — not with dread, but with wonder. Because who are we, that the Almighty would stoop to hear our whispers and answer with Heaven? Who are we, that He would take dust and breathe destiny into it? This next chapter is an invitation to pause and consider — to look back, remember, and revere the God who never stopped being good.

# CHAPTER XV - REVERENCE OF THE KING

As I sit here today and look back on the years marked by pain and poor choices, I can't help but feel a deep ache of embarrassment. I really put myself through all of that? What was I thinking?

I see the progress—but I also feel the pain. It's hard to pull myself out of the spiral of self-pity and look at the bigger picture. Hard to believe that something good could come from all of that mess. Because I lived it. I felt every moment. And when you're in the middle of your storm, it's nearly impossible to imagine that God is building a testimony out of the wreckage.

But isn't that just how it goes? We have such a hard time valuing what God values. We struggle to detach from our pain long enough to see how God is weaving purpose through it. But when we do—when we take even a step back—suddenly we can see it: His fingerprints over everything. His mercy, quiet and consistent. His protection, even when we were running.

What a faithful God we serve.

Only now can I truly see what He spared me from. Only now can I recognize how He orchestrated moments, people, and even my own failures to lead me back to Him. Only now can I appreciate the way He never gave up—even when I had.

And when I look at where I am now, the question still stirs: how did I get here? How did I move from being the person I was to the person I'm becoming? How did I escape the mess I made?

The answer is simple, but not easy. It started with the fear of the Lord.

See, back then, I was my own god. I decided what was right. I called the shots. I thought I could play with fire and not get burned. I thought I knew just enough about Jesus to be safe. But the truth? I didn't fear Him. I didn't honor Him. I didn't revere Him.

It wasn't until I was at my lowest—stripped of my confidence, my pride, my illusion of control—that the weight of His majesty broke through. That's when reverence finally took root. Not just fear in the trembling sense, but awe. Honor. Recognition of His holiness, His sovereignty, His mercy.

And everything changed.

If there's one thing I could urge you to hold onto, it's this: Never lose sight of who He is. He is holy. He is righteous. He is the Creator, the King, the Lord Almighty. Your life won't change because of willpower or self-help or motivation—it changes through surrender. And surrender is only real when it's grounded in reverence for Yahweh.

So spend time at His feet. Don't just ask for His hand—sit at His throne. A lifestyle of godly choices, of lasting change, is built on the foundation of fearing the Lord.

And one more thing—don't ever underestimate the power of your story.

Everything you've walked through, every failure and every victory, every tear and every breakthrough—it wasn't wasted. One day, your story might be the thing that draws someone else out of the dark. It might be the spark that brings another soul to repentance. It might be the very thing God uses to fulfill the Great Commission through you.

And if even one person comes to Jesus because of what you've endured?

Then it was all worth it. Every single bit.

# A MESSAGE FROM THE AUTHOR

I didn't write this book for attention, nor applause, nor a profit. I wrote it because I had to—because I couldn't stay silent. I wrote it from a place of deep compassion and unshakable conviction.

If you've made it this far, I want to speak directly to you.

Maybe you're reading this while carrying a secret or wrestling with shame behind closed doors, just like I once did. I know the weight, I know the fear, but I also know the freedom that's waiting for you on the other side.

Here's what I learned in my struggle, something that could change everything for you; bring it into the light. Tell someone and confess your sin. Scripture says, "Confess your sins to one another and pray for one another, that you may be healed."

You weren't meant to do this alone. If you can't find the strength to make the right decisions, then find someone who will walk with you. Someone who won't let you settle for less than what God has for you. Someone who will lead you, not to themselves, but to Jesus.

Because only Jesus can save, only Jesus can restore, and only Jesus can set you free.

This book was never meant to scare you, but it is meant to wake you up. There is a real heaven and there is a real hell. A flame of sin that consumes and a holy fire that purifies.
Will it be the fire of destruction or the fire of refinement? Will it be the flame of self-will, or the flame of surrender?

The choice is in your hands.
The question is simple: Which flame has your consent to burn?

# ABOUT THE AUTHOR

Aidan Lambert is an evangelist, missionary, author, and the founder and president of Lambert Ministries, a global evangelistic movement with a clear mission: to win all of the Americas for Jesus. Aidan's heart burns with the message of surrender, holiness, and the power of the Gospel to transform lives. But his passion didn't come from theory, it came from fire.

Once walking in quiet rebellion, masking spiritual emptiness with religious familiarity, Aidan knows what it means to be bound and broken. Though he grew up in church, it wasn't until he came face-to-face with the mercy and majesty of Jesus that everything changed. It was grace that found him, truth that broke him, and love that rebuilt him. From the ashes of compromise, he rose, not perfect, but wholly surrendered.

Today, Aidan travels city to city, nation to nation, carrying a mandate to awaken hearts, disciple the Church, and call this generation to choose the flame of holiness over the fires of sin. Through Lambert Ministries, he and his team pour into churches, young adults, leaders, and the lost, teaching them not only how to burn for God, but how to burn rightly.

His life and calling are not about platforms, but altars and not about performance but presence. With every sermon preached, every soul saved, and every page written, Aidan's mission remains the same: to bring the nations, especially the Americas, back to the feet of Jesus.

# ABOUT OUR MINISTRY

Lambert Ministries is a global evangelistic ministry committed to igniting hearts with the transforming power of the Gospel. Founded by evangelists Aidan and Faith Lambert, our mission is to see lives radically changed by Jesus Christ through street evangelism, church ministry, and both international and domestic missions. We are passionate about witnessing genuine moves of God wherever we go, with a particular focus on reaching the Americas. Our vision is to lead the Body of Christ back to their first love, cultivating a burning passion for the presence of God. We believe in the importance of making disciples of all nations, fulfilling the Great Commission by coming alongside believers on their journey of faith.

To support this mission, we established the Next Steps discipleship ministry, designed to equip and guide individuals in their  spiritual growth with four components: our Discipleship Course, 15-Day Bible Reading Plan, our Life Coach program, and church locator form. You can learn more about Next Steps and how you can partner with us or get involved at www.lambertministries.org/nb.

 Recognizing the vital role of unity in the Kingdom, especially among worship leaders and musicians, we created the Levites Worship Alliance. This initiative fosters covenant relationships with musicians across the USA, promoting harmony and collaboration in worship. Discover more at www.lambertministries.org/levites.

For additional information about our ministry and how you can get involved, please visit www.lambertministries.org.

Made in the USA
Columbia, SC
14 November 2025

72548880R00075